Tiny Tinkles Little Musicians Series

Little Composers

Activity Book I
Tracing Letters, Notes and Symbols

Created by **Debra Krol** Pictures by **Corinne Orazietti**

This book is dedicated to
all the little people for inspiring me,
and all the BIG people for believing in me.

Copyright © 2021 Tiny Tinkles Publishing Company

All Rights Reserved.

No parts of this publication or the characters in it, may be reproduced or distributed in any form or by any means without written permission from the publisher.

To request permission, or for school visits and book readings, please visit www.tinytinkles.com

ISBN (Paperback Perfect Bound): 978-0-9808888-7-4

First Edition 2021

Ally Alligator

Ally Alligator LOVES the letter **A!**

Ally Alligator LOVES the color **PURPLE**

Ally Alligator SINGS **CHOMP**

Trace Ally Alligator's Favorite Letter

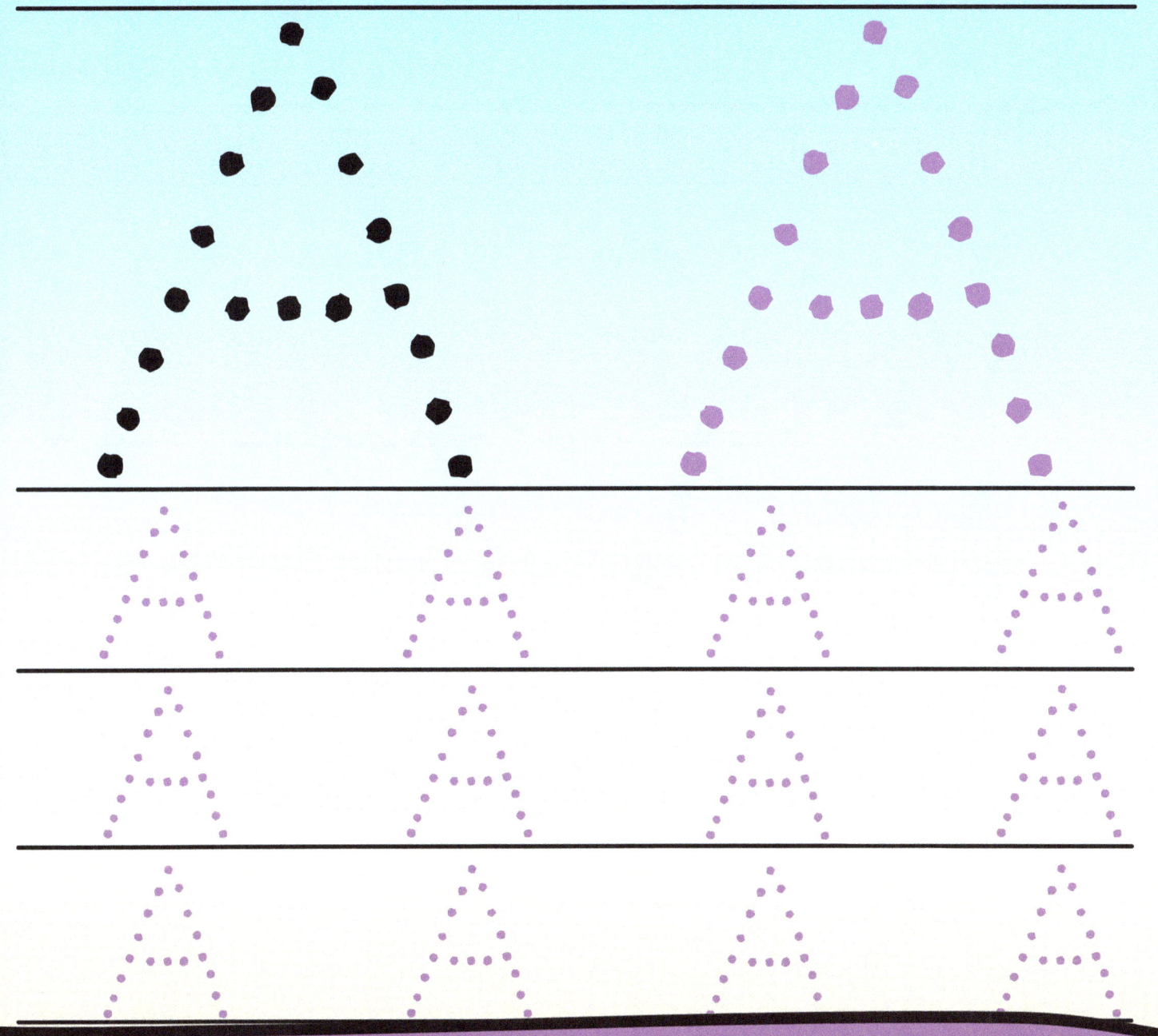

Brownie Bear

Brownie Bear LOVES the letter B!

Brownie Bear LOVES the color PINK

Brownie Bear SINGS ROAR

Trace Brownie Bear's Favorite Letter

Trace Chloe Cat's Favorite Letter

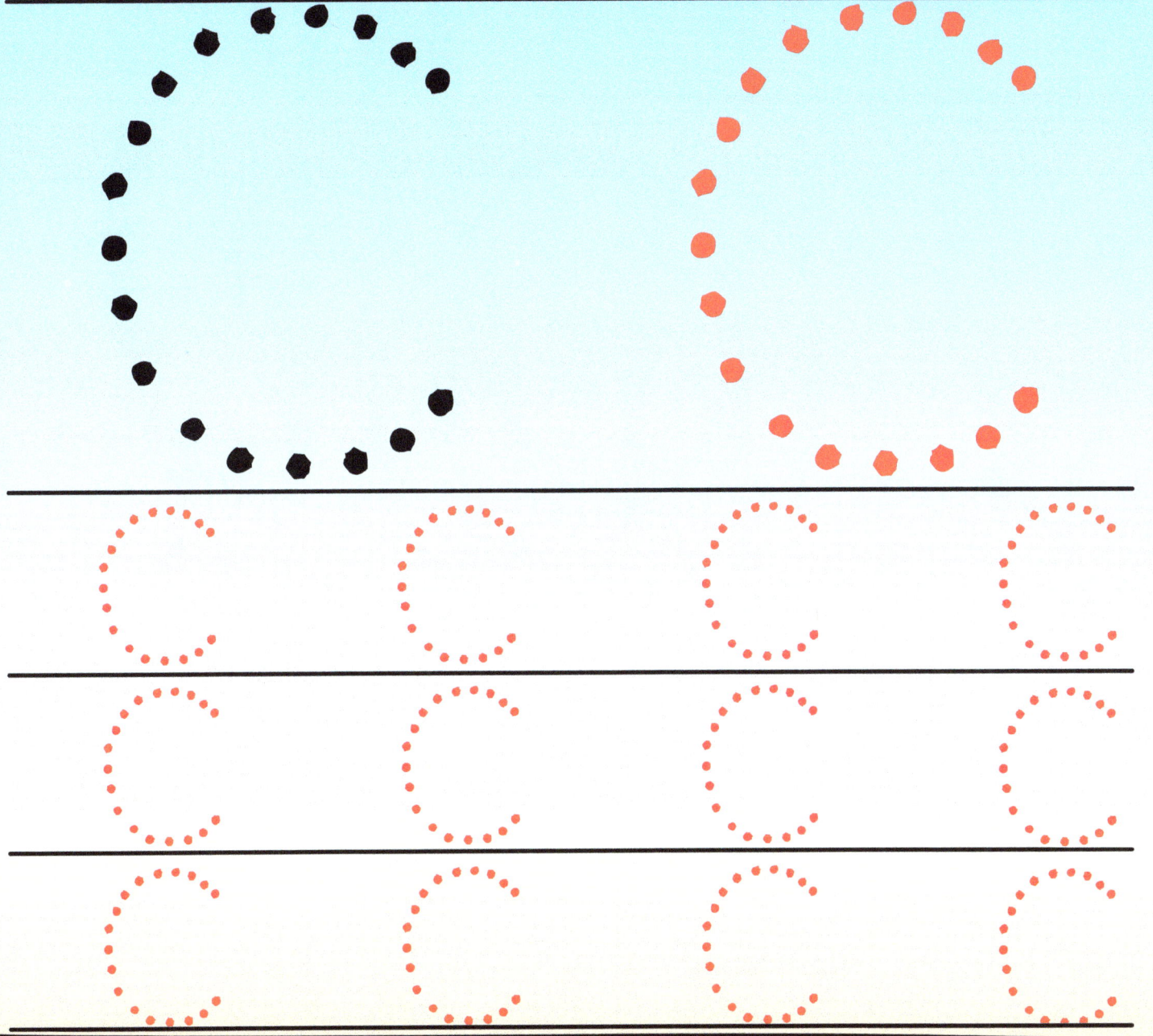

DAISY DOG

Daisy Dog LOVES the letter D!

Daisy Dog LOVES the color ORANGE

Daisy Dog SINGS WOOF

Elly Elephant

Elly Elephant LOVES the letter E!

Elly Elephant LOVES the color YELLOW

Elly Elephant SINGS PAH WOO

Trace Elly Elephant's Favorite Letter

Franky Frog

Franky Frog LOVES the letter **F!**

Franky Frog LOVES the color **GREEN**

Franky Frog SINGS **RIBBIT**

Trace Franky Frog's Favorite Letter

Gordie Goat

Gordie Goat LOVES the letter G!

Gordie Goat LOVES the color BLUE

Gordie Goat SINGS MAA

Trace Gordie Goat's Favorite Letter

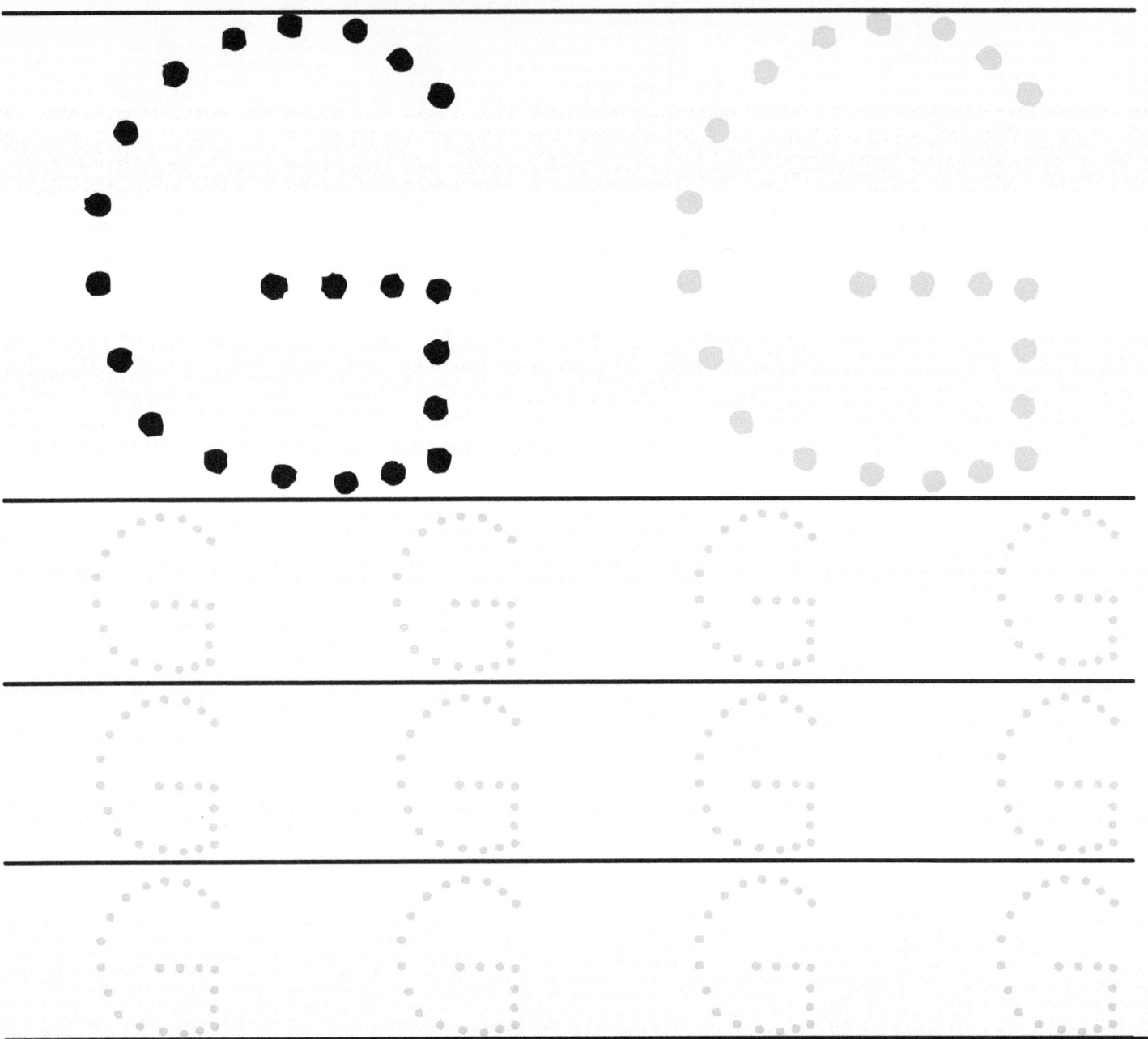

trace your

Rosie Rabbit
Missy Mouse
Parker Penguin
Pokey Porcupine
Tommy Thumb

Tommy Thumb

Tommy Thumb LOVES the Number 1

Tommy Thumb is a CAT

Tommy Thumb SINGS MEOW MEOW Number 1

Trace Tommy Thumb's Favorite Number

Parker Penguin

Parker Penguin LOVES the Number 2

Parker is a Penguin

Parker Penguin SINGS DOOT DOOT Number 2

Trace Parker Penguin's Favorite Number

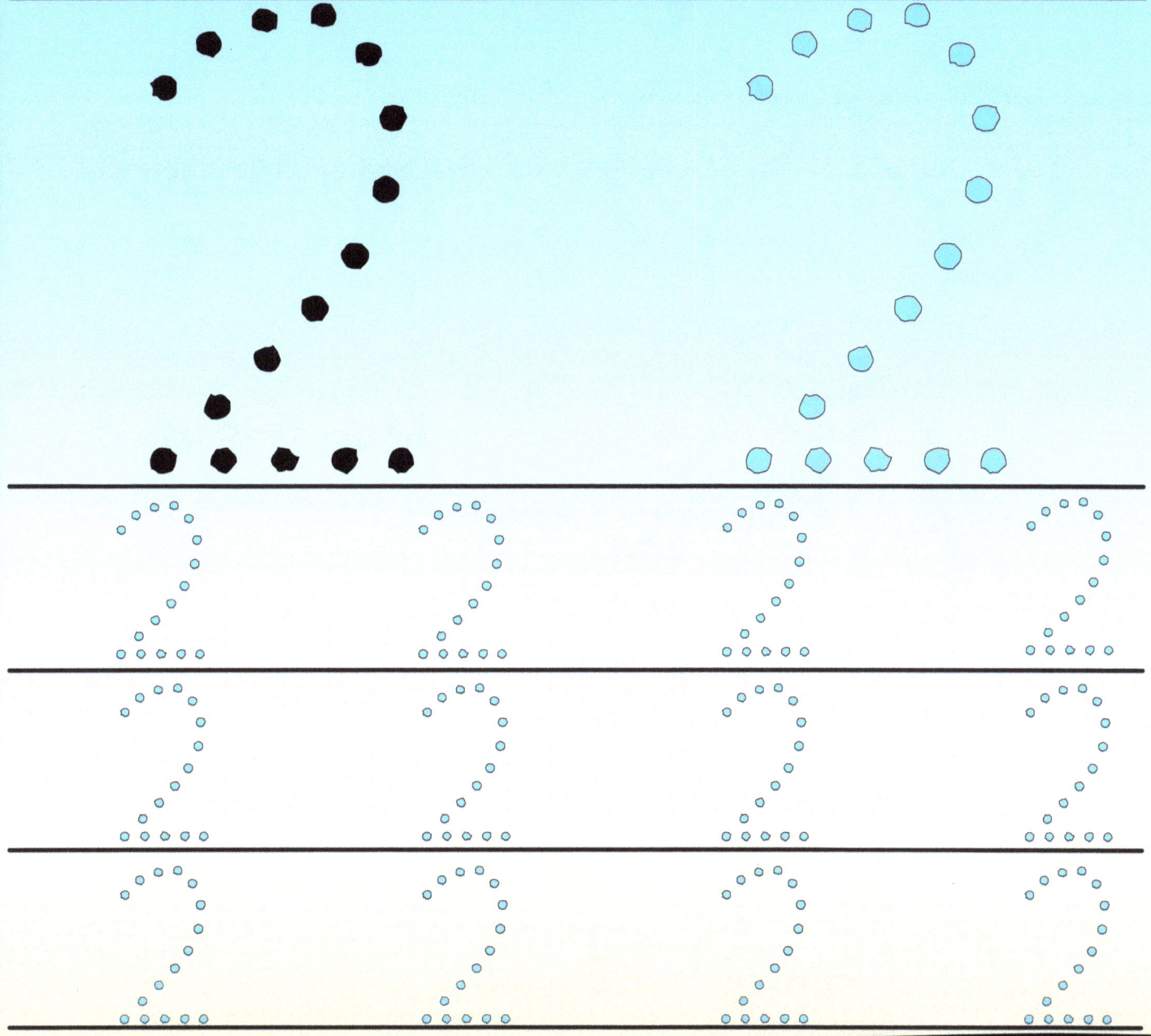

Missy Mouse

Missy Mouse LOVES the Number 3

Missy is a Mouse

Missy Mouse SINGS SQUEAK SQUEAK Number 3

Trace Missy Mouse's Favorite Number

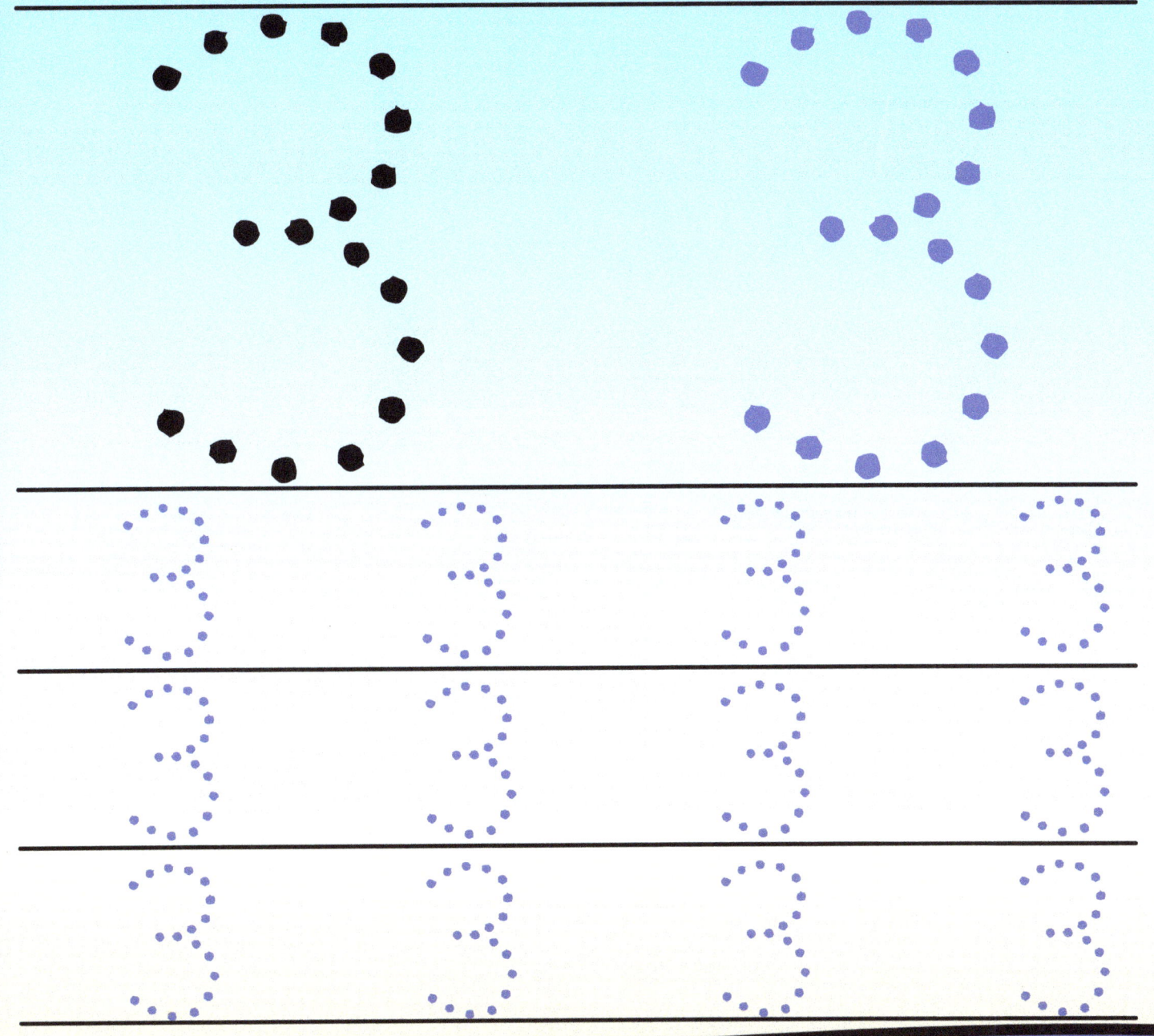

Rosie Rabbit

Rosie Rabbit LOVES the **Number 4**

Rosie is a **Rabbit**

Rosie Rabbit SINGS HOP HOP **Number 4**

Trace Rosie Rabbit's Favorite Number

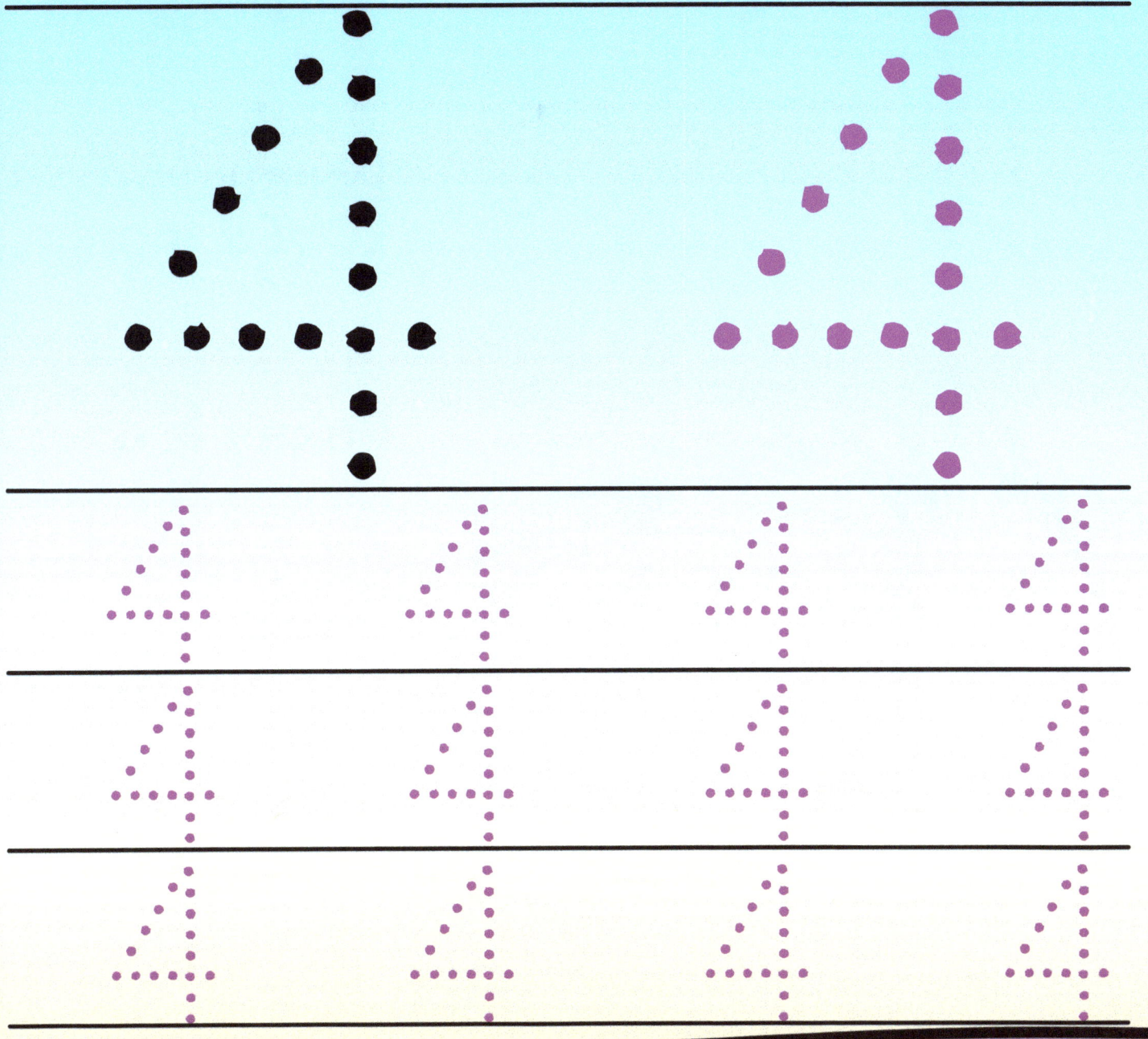

Pokey Porcupine

Pokey Porcupine LOVES the Number 5

Pokey is a Porcupine

Pokey Porcupine SINGS POKE POKE Number 5

Trace Pokey Porcupine's Favorite Number

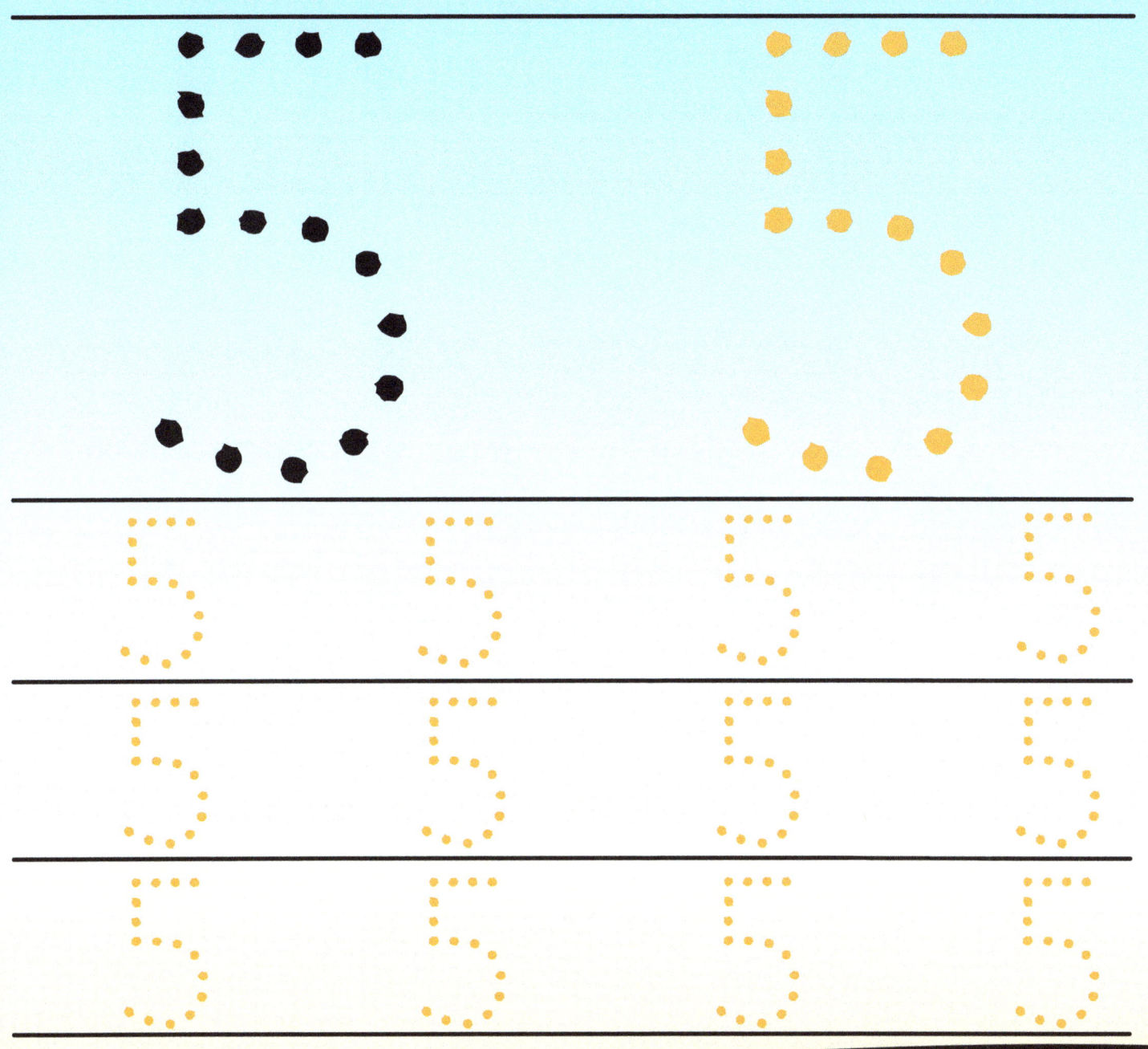

Kip The Quarter Note

I'm Kip! ¼ is my favorite number!

Kip's Quarter Note Song

Round and round the notes are round.

Add a stem, is it Up or Down?

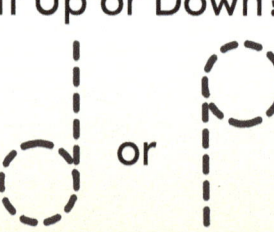 or

Quarter Notes are colored in. KIP the quarter note is colored in.

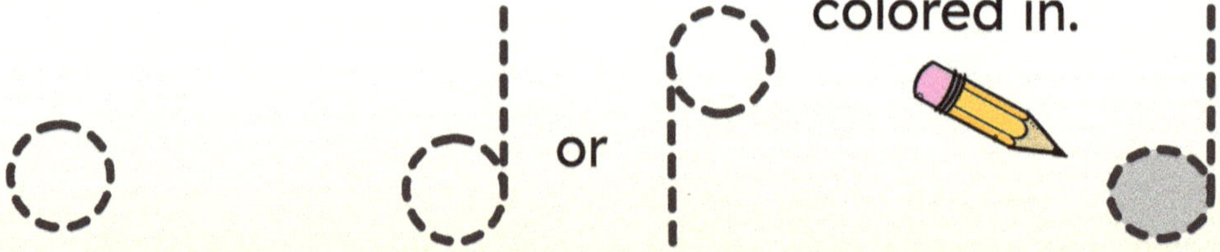

Trace and color all the quarter notes. Point to each one and count 1.

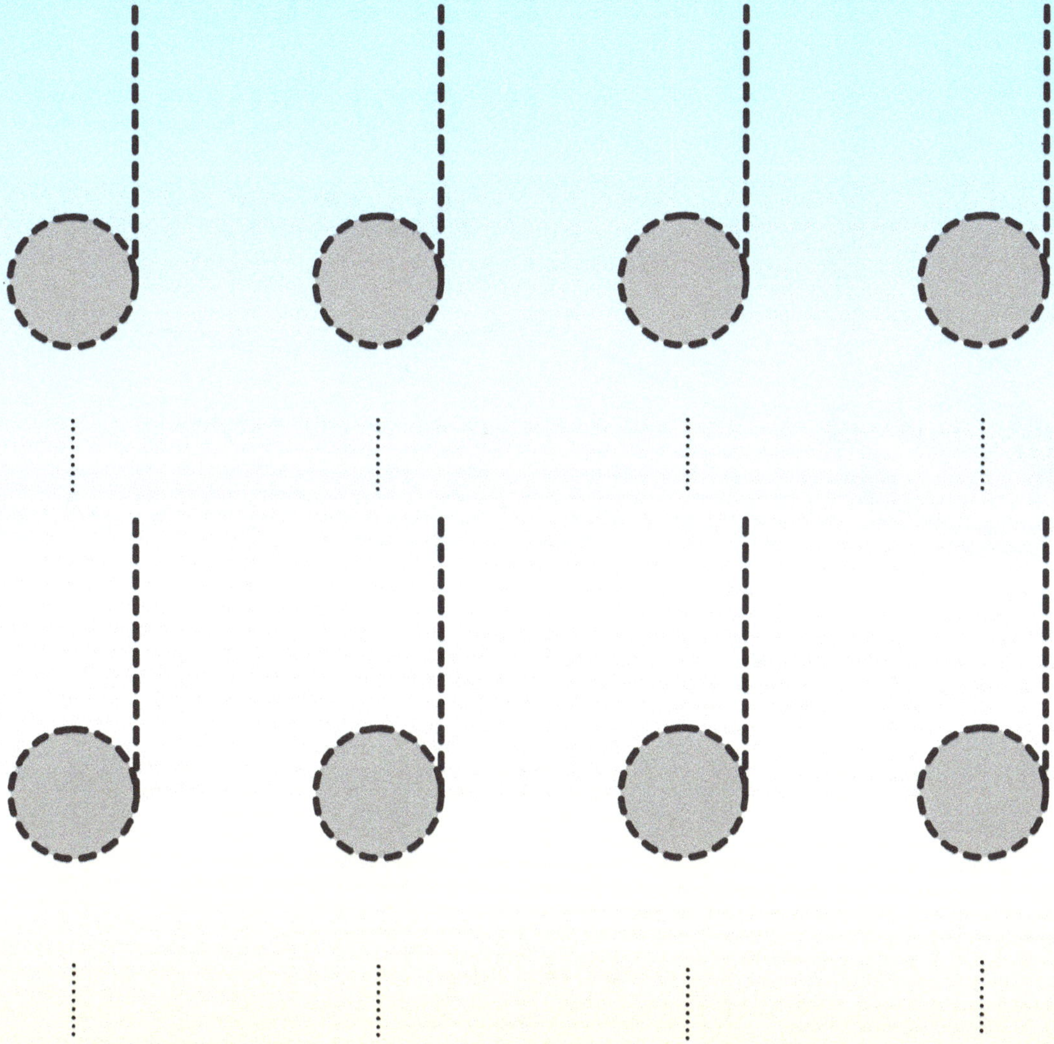

Hugo The Half Note

I'm Hugo! 2 is my favorite number!

Hugo's Half Note Song

Round and round the notes are round.

Add a stem, is it Up or Down?

Hugo the half note, holds on tight. Hugo's favorite color is white.

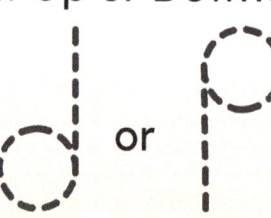

Trace all the half notes.
Point to each one and count 1-2.

Silly Willy The Whole Note

Silly Willy's Whole Note Song

Round and round the notes are round.

Silly Willy is getting dizzy.

Silly Willy is really long!
1 2 3 4 he sings his song.

 Trace all of the whole notes.
Point to each one and count 1-2-3-4.

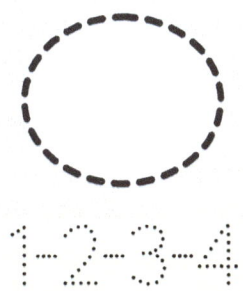 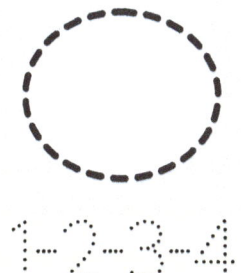

Grammy Treble Clef

Grammy Treble Clef loves to sing the HIGH NOTES. La la la la la, and we draw her just like this....

Grampy Bass Clef

Grampy Bass Clef loves to sing LOW NOTES. Du du du du du and we draw him just like this....

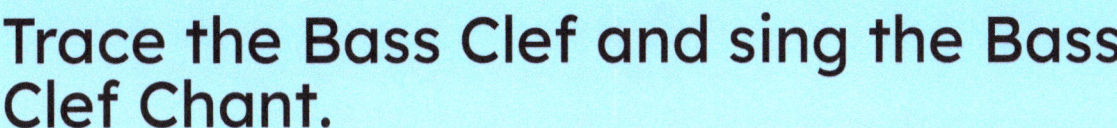

Trace the Bass Clef and sing the Bass Clef Chant.

Round and round the circle, let's draw Grampy's Ear.

Round and round and round and round, two dots on the side.

 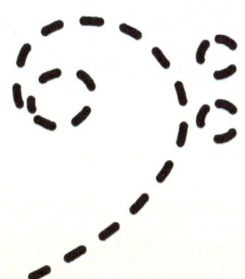  

Mr. Repeat

Mr. Repeat Loves to HEAR you play! Wait a minute, what did you say? Can you please play it again!

 Trace color in all of the Repeat Signs.

Mr. Fermata

CALM...   AHH...
Mr. Fermata, loves taking
deep breaths
CALM...   AHH...
he loves to PAUSE.

 **Trace and color in all of the Fermata Signs.**

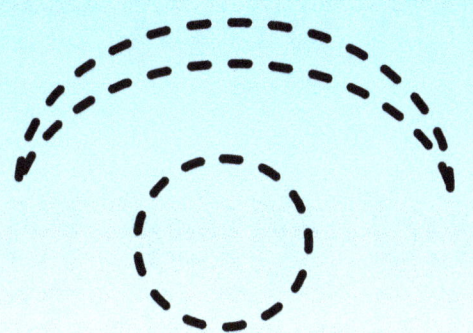 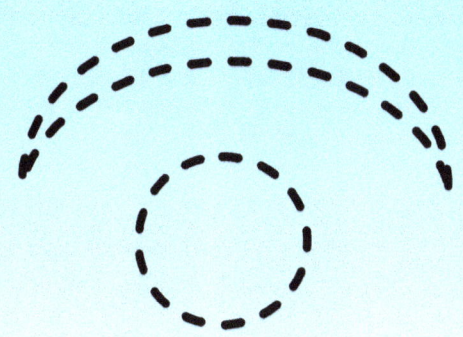

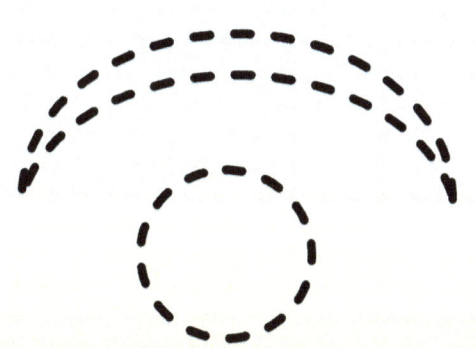 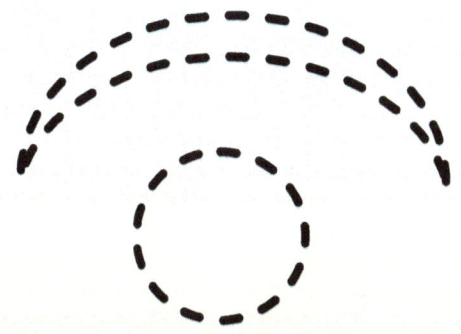

Mr. Fine

Mr. Fine always says GOODBYE.

And when the song is over, he says his name...

FINE.

THE END.

 Trace and color in all of the Fine signs.

ABOUT THE CREATORS

Debra Krol is a BC Registered Music Teacher who specializes in teaching music to babies, toddlers and preschoolers. She is also a children's songwriter and author. Ms. Deb enjoys camping with her hubby, kids, and Daisy Dog, their black and tan coonhound. She loves playing piano, ukulele, guitar and most of all, singing & drawing with all of her little friends!

 Tiny Tinkles Music Studio   tinytinkles

Corinne Orazietti was a preschool and elementary teacher for many years. She saw how her whimsical illustrations added sparkle to her lessons and decided it was time to share her passion for art with others. She now works as a full-time artist at her company, Chirp Graphics, and spends her days drawing cartoon dragons and fairies.

 chirpgraphics   chirpgraphicsclipart

ABOUT THIS SERIES

The Tiny Tinkles Little Musicians Series was created to help little musicians experience the FUN of learning music. Every book in the Little Musician series features a Story to read, Songs to sing and play, and a ton of fun Games to play together! When a child plays to learn, they learn to play.

More books in the Little Musician Series Available in 2021.

CONGRATULATIONS!

_____
Student's Name

Has completed Level I Little Composer
In the Tiny Tinkles Little Musician Series.

LEVEL I

_____
Teacher

_____
Date

www.ingramcontent.com/pod-product-compliance
Lightning Source LLC
Chambersburg PA
CBHW061816290426
44110CB00026B/2883